My *View*

Kitiara Weaver

PAGE PUBLISHING
Conneaut Lake, PA

First originally published by Page Publishing 2024

ISBN 979-8-89157-167-9 (pbk)
ISBN 979-8-89157-182-2 (digital)

Printed in the United States of America

To a very special person in my life who has
done nothing but help, support, and encourage
me to publish my work!

Contents

The Coldness

The coldness comes closer
The numbness goes deeper
It plays her like a composer
Knowing she's a keeper
Cannot stop it
From coming for her
It will make her submit
It comes from nowhere
Cannot stop her from going
Or hide from the fear
That continues growing
The walls block off
Access to her heart
Surrounded by a trough
It'll keep her apart
Not letting her think
About anything good
So instead, she shrink
Because she's never understood.

Letting Go

Never ready
To let go
Have to stay steady
Because you know
The pain will come
And bring you low
Where it comes from
You already know
It wants you
To give up
You can't get through
A sip of a cup
To end the life
Or a slice
Of a knife
That is precise
If the pain comes
And you let it stay
It causes numbs
It'll have its way.

Darkness

Lost in the darkness
That swallows you whole
It'll turn you into a carcass
That it can control
To the very end
It'll stake a claim
You can try to defend
Or pass the blame
To survive it
You must fight daily
Or you'll submit
To the whispering gaily
Even when dead
The darkness will come
It is said
With a quiet hum
Everything is at stake
So find that light
In the wake
And hold it tight.

Confusion

The confusion surrounds
Always making us question
All those bounds
With so many suggestions
It becomes a loop
That feels never-ending
One that can stoop
All confusion is depending
Whether it'll go away
If it can be cleared
One must say
And face what's feared
No little task
No little fet
To remove the mask
That confusion threat
To keep in place
To speak your voice
Will help replace
The confusing choice.

Improving Mood

No matter the mood
You can lighten it
Anger subdued
Happiness lit
Adding a new view
A place of safety
Everything pure and true
Nothing has to be hasty
A space of vulnerability
But also with strength
A complete stability
That comes in length
So much tenderness
Is held between us
With a gentleness
That's knee-weakening, thus
Call it fate
Written in the sky
That is create
In a blink of an eye.

My Advice

It's so easy
To lose the breezy
To let it upset
And make us
Question everything
There's little to discuss
When you use to carrying
Everything alone
It can be scary
Of the unknown
A little wary
Of the path
You must walk
Where there's no wrath
One must talk
Not in a letter
So my advice
Is face the fear
It's worth the price
Everything will be clear.

Should It Be a Surprise?

The first meet
Causing excitement
And no retreat
It is consignment
But should it be
A keep surprise
To fully see
Light in those eyes
Or should I tell
My plan for you
One I compel
To follow through
How would you
Feel about a surprise
If only I knew
Your replies
Yet this I know
I hold no fear
Ready to undergo
This journey, dear.

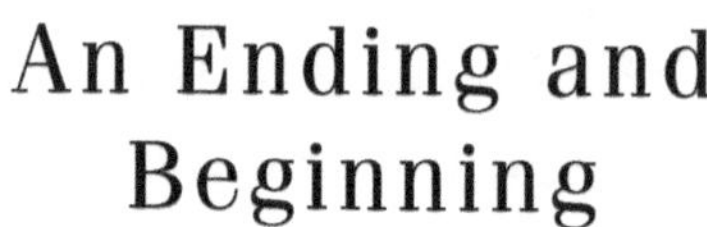

An Ending and Beginning

One door closes
Another one opens
One can be exposed
From all the emotions
What no one tells
Are those goodbyes
Breaks the shells
So you can rise
They don't say
How free it feels
On that day
How it reveals
A new world ahead
New journeys to take
Instead, it's said
How much one break
As it ends
No one said
That it depends
If you were misled
And maybe it offends

Those not involved
Those who don't know
Why it dissolved
Why you let go
To let yourself feel
Happiness and delight
That is real
Because it's right.

Adventures

New adventures
Await ahead
Some ventures
Fill us with dread
While one
Fills us with strength
Like warmth from the sun
Helping us in length
In this new beginning
And energy that bursts
So many of them
Made me scared
I thought condemn
'Cause no one cared
Now it's untrue
And I know it
Because of you
The love emit
Between us
Brings the best
And so thus
There's nothing stressed.

Dreams

Images flash
Throughout my dreams
A fire with no ash
A light that gleams
All—cause a warmth
All are a desire
To lose north
And climb higher
Only one
Is the star
It just begun
Now we're afar
But the dream
Of the meeting
It all seem
To be sweeting
The anxiety leaves
Replaced with keenness
As the mind conceives
The uniqueness
Of what it held

To still come
It is compelled
To still form them.

A Wish

Every night I wished
Upon the star
Not once was missed
Could it hear so far
Hope was lost
Yet still, I did
At all cost
Yet it hid
Looking back now
I wasn't ready
Didn't hear the vow
To stay steady
I dreamed of
Someone who accepted
Me with love
To be selected
For me above
The time arrived
For my wish hereof
To be revived
As it came true

Better than expected
It gave me you
And love unconditioned.

The Reason Why

Behind every emotion
There is a reason
A little notion
Toward the season
There is one
That stands strong
That I feel for
That feels to belong
Behind this adore
I know why
This feeling grew
I cannot deny
You are caring
And sweet
Oh, so daring
In this heat
You seem fearless
In front of a crowd
So often, I'm speechless
The glimpse allowed
All of this.

Time

It is okay
To say no
There will be a day
This I know
There is time
So let's not hast
Let it climb
Let it last
If not now
Then another day
While the how
May confuse, I say
It will come
When it's right
For it to become
A new height
It's worth the wait
When it's true
So the date
Between the two
To finally meet

Will be
Perfect and complete
Between you and me.

Why Do I Try?

Why do I try?
It is never right
In your eye
It's always a fight
Always so wrong
Never getting easier
To stay so strong
Life isn't breezier
Why do I try?
Nobody cares
When I cry
And shed tears
Nothing changes
Never gets easier
There are no exchanges
Nothing is breezier
Why do I try?
No one pays attention.
So I ask why
Do I mention
Never gets easier

Expecting no reply
There's nothing breezier
I cannot deny.

Choices

Here I sit
Torn between choices
Wondering what could be
And what currently is
Can we fix the past?
Or more the mistakes
We have made
Can we be happy
While we love each other
Are we still in love
And if not
Can we find it?
Am I torturing myself
Making life perfect for you
Yet miserable for myself
You feel peace
I feel unsettled
You feel safe
I feel scared
You feel cared for
And I feel ignored.

A Fairy Tale

Through all the pain
And misery intertwined
There was no complain
Nothing else to find
Never truly believed
Deserving any better
Nothing else received
Nothing else for her
Stuck to the pattern
The same abuse
Until a turn
Was introduce
Completely unexpected
Showing the truth
Two were connected
And restored was youth
He showed her
A new light
Deserving she were
Bringing about delight
A happily ever

Blessed upon two
Through a new endeavor
A fairy tale true.

Hello

To me
The goodbye
Shall never be
If asked why
The answer is easy
Because I believe
While it may be cheesy
That love receive
And given truly
Along with truth
And trust absolutely
It brings a soothe
Along with a peace
To fully know
Believe the release
So completely show
The emotions inside
And be brave
There's nothing to hide
Accept what's gave
And given back fully

Then you'll know
Truly and surely
There is only hello.

Why Am I Here?

Why am I here?
With the constant pain
That is severe
And constantly remain
Emotionally distressed
With no ease in sight
No time to rest in the middle of the night
Why am I here?
Always with an ache
That never seems to clear
Never taking a break
It cannot be filled
With no ease in sight
Because it can't be willed
Into the night
Why am I here?
With no heart to give
And no one to hear
Or a reason to live
With no love to have
With no ease in sight

Because of the halve
Left here tonight
Why am I here?
A broken soul
And everything unclear
Never to be whole
I cannot be fixed
With no ease in sight
Because everything is mixed
It'll end this night.

Ray

Excitement spins
Around the air
As everything begins
Remember, it's rare
To begin a new
To count the days
Down into a few
To meet the ray
That brings change
In the best way
Dream of the exchange
Of heat ablaze
No fear of burn
From the fire lit
As you'll learn
When it fit
There's nothing better
The future days
Nothing sweeter
Than your rays.

Say No

I'll understand
If you say no
I won't demand
Just want to know
What you're thinking
What goes on
While I'm sinking
Is it foregone
Am I fooling
Myself and heart
Am I cooling
The heat from start
Is it real
Or just a game
Can you reveal
The true flame
I wish I knew
That you wanted
Me, like I do you
I feel we're bonded
But is it true?

Responses confuse
Should I pursue
What do you choose?

Fated

So close to you
Yet still far away
If only I knew
The right way
The strength it takes
To not grab keys
Chase what makes
These dreams that tease
To meet the reason
Behind the smile
That has woken
My sleeping heart, while
Showing me the beauty
All from afar
Just proves absolutely
That fated we are
It will continue to grow
Sweeter by the day
Causing a bright glow
That will stay.

Words...

The words are hard
Not good at this
Usually disregard
Always dismiss
So often feel
The words are wrong
They don't reveal
They don't prolong
Like they're meant to
They bring it down
If only a way
Around this
To truly say
Would be bliss
Yet words are hard
Unless this way
To let down my guard
And fully display.

Today

Today is your day
And you're gone
How can I say
Now you're withdrawn
How much I miss you
How much you did
None of us knew
All this you hid
Your shoes unfilled
The piece missing
Everything is chilled
All feel dismissing
You left too soon
So much missed
It is only June
It's all a misled
Without you here
Any celebration
Brings many tear
To that participation
Know you are loved

And missed dearly
You'll always be beloved
So deep and sincerely.

My Child

I watched you grow
Standing beside you
Supporting you through
Because I knew
You'd be strong
Beautiful and independent
You'd find where you belong
You are transcendent
How proud of you
I could never express
The lady you grew into
What I never guess
Was the day
You no longer needed
Me to clear the way
You have succeeded
In everything
You put your mind to
The beauty you bring
Continue to be true
Follow your heart

As I continue to see
You, even apart
Who you will be.

Nature

The feel of the sand
Or the cool breeze
It's hard to understand
The happiness of these
The solitude it brings
How it can open one's mind
To new things
To help remind
Us of the beauty around
I miss the feelings
Brought by the sound
They cause healings
Whether it's a lake
Or mountain or ocean
Your breath it'll take
From the powerful emotion
That the beauty
Will stir within you
How free of duty
From the view
Absolute freedom felt

Escaping reality
This beauty dealt
Wrapped in hospitality.

Blue Eyes

Everywhere I look
I see blue
Once was all it took
To see the new
Beautiful and bright
Matching the sky
Down to the light
I don't try
To remove it
From my mind
I can only admit
What I find
Truth behold
The color blue
Has a hold
On me anew
A changing color
Can match the ocean
Like no other
It can hold devotion
Beauty and light

Nothing can compare
To the sight
Of blue, I swear.

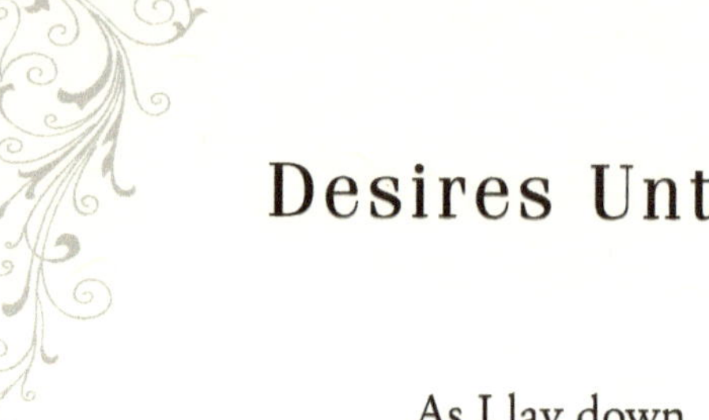

Desires Untold

As I lay down
In bed to sleep
My mind goes around
With images to keep
With my eyes
Completely closed
I am surprised
By what's composed
How this mind
Can produce so clear
Images designed
With such sincere
How it knows
My desires untold
How it grows
That hold
On my heart
That now belongs
With this new start.

Why Do You Talk to Me?

Sometimes I wonder why
You talk to me
When you're the perfect guy
Many would agree
I'm not good with words
Unsure what to say
Always losing my nerves
My point I can't convey
Do you understand
That I cherish
Your time and
Don't want this to perish
Yet you are on my mind
Constantly and all I
Want is to confined
The truth but I'm shy
What would you say
If I said I like you
You make my day
If you knew

I think your handsome
Would you prefer perfect
That you're more than some
If you knew the effect
You had on me
That you're behind the smile
Without words, can you see
I'd go the mile
To keep you in my life
But how do I tell you
That while I may be a wife
From a view
Maybe I'm a terrible person
Thinking this way
But it only worsens
Not to say
So much to you
Would you stay
If I told you a few
Of them today?

Repay Love

What other way
Can you repay love
Other than say
The truth of
It all
To just be you
And stand tall
Because that is
All that one needs
For it says
Love to succeeds
What other way
Do you repay love
On this day
With a clear sky above
Than to be you
Everyday
To be true
With every word you say.

Your Smile

The words slip out
So easily off my tongue
I have no doubt
That among
Everything else
To see you smile
It makes me melts
All the while
Wanting you to be happy
To bring you peace
Maybe I'm sappy
There needs to be release
I know I say
I'm sorry too much
On this day
I mean it in such
A way to show
How much I care
I want you to know
There's no unclear air
Between the two of us

Because what you mean
To me is as thus
It must have been.

The Door

There is beauty
Behind the door
Without any duty
To rage a war
It was cracked
And left open
Meant to attract
Those broken
Everyone has one
That comes at a time
When you're left spun
Like a dime
Behind the door
Is nothing but joy
And so much more
Never a decoy
One must close
The previous chapter
To find the most
Without a captor
Because behind the door

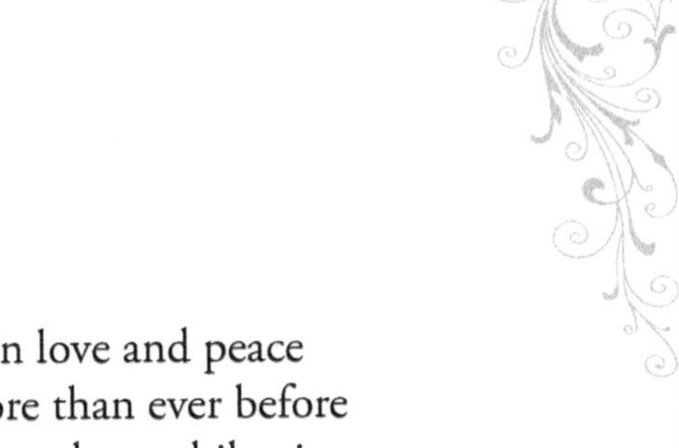

In love and peace
More than ever before
You can be a while piece.

Change

The changes you bring
Brought light to my life
Like a blooming spring
In the middle of a strife
An angel from above
To help find the light
To show the truth of love
Something to hold tight
Giving the strength
To face challenges
Even those at length
In everything this life
Throws in the way
Even if it's a rife
To see a new day
Much joy and love
Wrapped in safety
Letting us fly like a dove
Nothing has to be hasty
So much time ahead
Don't hear the challenges to face

Nowhere else, instead
To rather be
Unless it was closer to you
But maybe it's just me
Yet do you feel it too?

New View

A gentle push
In a new direction
To not hide in a bush
To see a further reflection
To open eyes
And fix connections
All the broken ties
No more seeing imperfections
All because of you
Helping me see
A different view
All of this is free
A change of perspective
A better look
With a new objective
Is all it took
For a new view
To come into place
So thank you
For the embrace.

A New

A new day
To begin again
Try what may
Nothing can stop when
A new light
Appears ahead
To bring sight
To the path unled
A new way
Of a better life
Is on display
With no strife
A new night
Calls to me
To take flight
To be free
A new view
Is all it takes
To wake to
What's at stakes
A new love

To make a smile
Sent from above
Helps that extra mile.

Better for Me

The path ahead
Holds so much light
With no one to lead
Away from the sight
Hold your head high
You can breathe freely
And know why
It's obvious, really
Enjoying life
The smile on your face
Cut free with a knife
To finally embrace
The beauty to see
The path you choice
As it should be
Let your voice
Be heard again
No one who gets mad
To say when
To be glad
At peace with yourself

Choose the best
For your heart itself
It can be expressed.

The Dark

Even in darkness
You shine bright
There's no harshness
Leading to the light
You make the dark
Disappear from sight
With one remark
Every single night
It cannot touch
When you fight
With strength, so much
The dark despite
The worst days
Hold no bite
With your phrase
Everything is delight
So simple words
Break walls into thirds
Never to reunite
Every single day
And even tonight

One must say
Dark cannot stand white
And in this
You're the knight
That creates bliss
To hold tight.

When I Break

The darkening sky
Matches my mood
Everything passes by
So I conclude
I hold her
I help him
And what for
Because it's grim
I hold it in
To be strong
As it's been
All along
When I cry
Who will hold me
They all rely
For me to be
Strong and there
Yet when I break
No one is aware
Of my ache.

Only One

When things turn gray
Your world upside down
There is a ray
To turn you around
Something goes wrong
Only one to tell
Will help you be strong
Don't say farewell
When everything is great
Only one to tell
Never want to wait
He can know as well
Yet on days
No news to share
There are still ways
To show we care
Though all of it
There is only one
You must admit
Where you can run.

Peace

The beauty of it all
Wraps around me
I can't recall
Last time I was free
A feeling of peace
Envelopes around me
Everything else release
They must agree
That the sight
In front of us
This very night
Is just a plus
To share the view
Of my world
To someone like you
Has me twirled
Wondering your thoughts
About everything around
All your wants
Yet to be found.

First Date

The blue sky above
Wind blowing your hair
Sharing the moment in love
To a place where
The world is quiet
Out in nature
All in private
All the greater
By the scene ahead
As the sun sets
With everything said
And no threats
The trail to there
Was worth the wait
This is rare
Chance of fate
It doesn't matter
If we sit on a blanket
Or tailgate chatter
No need for a jacket
With a beautiful sunset

And you beside me
There's no regret
Because perfect it will be.

Free

I look up at the sky
A smile on my face
I can't deny
The beauty of the place
The feeling of peace
Brought upon me
From the release
To finally be free
To be seen
For the real me
To see the scene
What could be
To love and be loved
To feel safe and secured
No need to be shoved
But to be reassured
With a desire
That burns
Longs to be acquired
What one learns
From standing by the fire

As the flames grow hotter
The common desire
Will have caught her.

Through Your Eyes

What would life be like
Through your eyes?
At the end of a hike
Looking at blue skies
To see the beauty
Around us, like you
To be off duty
If only I knew
The change in my life
That you created
You didn't need a knife
Because it was vacated
You brought happiness
Joy and love
Can't help the sappiness
Written here where of
With you, I am me
You see more than broken
I never thought it'd be
Yet I feel awoken
You are more to me

Without realizing it
Letting me be free
But I must admit
That I cannot deny
What I feel anymore
But how will you reply
If I open that door?

Horrible or
Deplorable?

Walls close in on me
There is one light
Could it be
You can make it right
The broken side
Could you mend
And not hide
Or make me pretend
You are safety
I can withstand
Yet can't be hasty
One does not understand
None was planned
Is it horrible
To admit the truth
Is it deplorable
I wasted my youth
You have me questioning
Why settle for less
It is welcoming

To fully express
Especially when one believes
They are falling for you
You could thieve
My heart with no clue.

Right Path

I compare the two
Paths in front of me
If only I knew
What was meant to be
As I look ahead
I picture my life
With nothing left unsaid
Because this rife
Has to end
So here I choose
To not pretend
There's no abuse
I'll leave this lie
Behind me
As I try
To finally be
Whom I need
Stop the wrath
And succeed
Down the right path.

The Place

I see the light.
Up ahead
It is bright.
Yet filled with dread.
It's perfect.
To be true
It has an effect.
Possible on you too
I feel fear.
For the unknown
Nothing is clear.
None has been shown.
The light is warmth.
Wrapping around me
Calling me thence fore
Come and see
The joy it brings.
By being set free
To hear those rings
The place meant to be.

About the Author

Kitiara Weaver, known to friends and family as Kiti, currently lives in Wyoming. She grew up between Utah and California before settling in Wyoming about five years ago. Writing has been a great pastime for Kiti. She has been writing all different genres and ideas for many years. However, the only one that stayed with her throughout the years was poetry. Kiti has a love for animals and nature. While she is constantly writing about her day or experiences throughout life, Kiti also works as a veterinarian technician. Those are her two main passions in life. At the age of twenty-eight, Kiti is divorced and has no biological children. She did take legal guardianship of her little sister and raise her. Kiti is always looking forward to new ideas and adventures. She spends her free time writing, taking her dogs up in the mountains, and spending time with family and friends.